Little Pebble™

KU-757-851

Transport

Trains

by Mari Schuh

raintree

a Capstone company — publishers for children

Raintree is an imprint of Capstone Global Library Limited, a company incorporated in England and Wales having its registered office at 264 Banbury Road, Oxford, OX2 7DY – Registered company number: 6695582

www.raintree.co.uk
myorders@raintree.co.uk

Edited by Carrie Braulick Sheely
Designed by Lori Bye
Picture research by Wanda Winch
Production by Katy LaVigne
Originated by Capstone Global Library Limited
Printed and bound in China

ISBN 978 1 4747 4431 7
21 20 19 18 17
10 9 8 7 6 5 4 3 2 1

British Library Cataloguing in Publication Data
A full catalogue record for this book is available from the British Library.

Acknowledgements
We would like to thank the following for permission to reproduce photographs: Alamy Stock Photo: Colin Underhill, 17, Jim West, 11; iStockphoto: BeyondImages, 15; Shutterstock: Albert Pego, 9, Bjorn Carlsson, 5, Dudarev Mikhail, 13, Frank Gaertner, 7, momente, 8, Sakarin Sawasdinaka, 21, Scanrail1, cover, Songquan Deng, 19, T. Sumaetho, zoom motion design

Every effort has been made to contact copyright holders of material reproduced in this book. Any omissions will be rectified in subsequent printings if notice is given to the publisher.

Contents

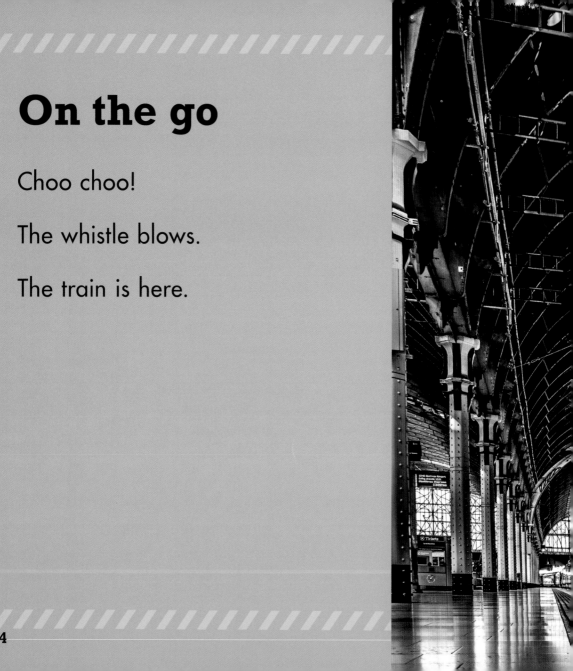

On the go

Choo choo!

The whistle blows.

The train is here.

All aboard!

People get into the train carraiges.

The train leaves the station.

Parts

Look at the front of the train.

This is the locomotive. It pulls the train.

The engine is inside. It makes power.

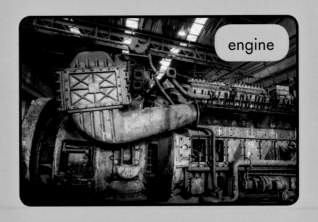
engine

locomotive

The cab is inside too.

The train driver sits in the cab.

He drives the train.

Look at the wheels.

They are made of steel.

They run on tracks.

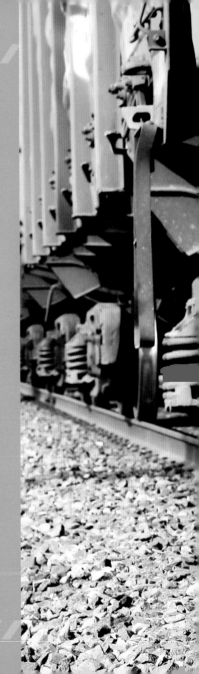

Types

A freight train carries goods.

It can carry coal.

Trains carry people to work.

They go into the city.

Some trains run under the ground.

They move under busy city streets.

Many people travel in them.

Way out ⟶

1 Morden
4 Morden   11:225

53683

A bullet train is fast and quiet.

It zooms by!

Are you ready for a train ride?

Glossary

cab   area where the train driver sits

engine   machine that makes the power needed to move something

locomotive   railway car that holds the engine to move the train

station   place where tickets for train journeys are sold and where people get on and off a train

steel   strong type of metal

track   set of steel rails that makes a path for trains

Find out more

Books

Big Machines Ride Rails! (Big Machines), Catherine Veitch (Raintree, 2015)

See Inside Trains (Usborne See Inside), Emily Bone (Usborne Publishing Ltd, 2013)

Trains (Usborne Beginners), Emily Bone (Usborne Publishing Ltd, 2011)

True or False? Transport, Dan Nunn (Raintree, 2014)

Websites

www.dkfindout.com/uk/transport/history-trains/
Learn the history of trains.

http://www.bbc.co.uk/education/clips/zpf34wx
Discover the importance of train travel in Victorian times.

Comprehension questions

1. How might people know that a train is coming?

2. What features make trains useful for carrying items?

3. In what ways do you think an underground system would be better than tracks that run above ground? In what ways could it be worse?

Index